A Day With An
Aztec

An Aztec

by Pablo Escalante Gonzalbo

Illustrations by Guillermo de Gante
Translated by Laura Dulin

RP

Runestone Press/Minneapolis
A Division of Lerner Publishing Group

All words that appear in **bold** are explained in the
glossary that starts on page 43.

This edition first published in the United States in 2000 by
Runestone Press.

Copyright © 1998 Editoriale Jaca Book spA, Milano. All rights reserved.
Originally produced in 1998 by Editoriale Jaca Book, Milan, Italy.

Runestone Press, a Division of Lerner Publishing Group
241 First Avenue North, Minneapolis, MN 55401 U.S.A.

Website: www.lernerbooks.com

Photos and artwork are used courtesy of Jaca Book, Milan, Italy: pp. 9 (bottom right), 10
(top left), 12 (top and bottom left), 13 (bottom left and top right), 14 (top right), 15; by
Daniela Balloni, p. 8 (bottom left and right), by Remo Berselli, p. 8-9, by Antonia
Maffeis, p. 9 (top right), by Angelo Stabin, p. 9 (top left); Museum of the Templo Mayor
and the National Museum of Anthropology, pp. 10 (bottom), 11; Salvador Guil'liem
Arroyo, pp. 12 (center), 13 (center), 14 (bottom); Illustration on page 14 (middle left)
was taken from Gisele Diaz and Alan Rogers. *The Codex Borgia, a Full-Color Restoration of
the Ancient Mexican Manuscript*, with an introduction and commentary by Bruce E. Byland
(New York: Dover Publications, 1993), p.61.

Library of Congress Cataloging-in-Publication Data

Esacalante, Pablo, 1963-
An Aztec / by Pablo Escalante Gonzalbo;
illustrations by Guillermo de Gante
p. cm.—(A day with)
Includes index.
Summary: Describes the history and customs of the Aztecs and concludes with a
fictionalized account of a young Aztec's experience in a battle against the Chalcas.
ISBN 0-8225-1921-6 (lib bdg: alk. paper)
1. Aztecs—Social life and customs Juvenile literature 2. Aztecs—Warfare
Juvenile literature. [1. Aztecs. 2. Indians of Mexico.] I. Title. II. Series
F1219.76.S64E73 2000
072—dc21   99-25325

Manufactured in the United States of America
1 2 3 4 5 6 – JR – 05 04 03 02 01 00

CONTENTS

INTRODUCTION

More than 10,000 years ago, bands of hunter-gatherers crossed a land bridge that then linked Asia to North America. By 7000 B.C., **Mesoamerica**—what would become Mexico, Guatemala, Belize, Honduras, and El Salvador—was home to hunter-gatherer societies. Mesoamerica extended into the deserts of northwestern Mexico. But most of the region was dense with vegetation. Highlands and mountains were covered with pine forests. Rivers flowed down from the mountains into **basins** and fed into lakes. Rain forests, thick jungles, broad savannas, and humid swamps dotted the warmer, wetter lowland areas.

People settled in small villages and began to practice agriculture. The Mesoamericans grew corn, beans, squash, and other foods. Deer, turkey, and rabbits provided wild game. Over time different languages, cultures, and religions arose. Crocodiles, jaguars, and poisonous snakes—animals of the region that posed dangers to humans—played roles in the mythology of many Mesoamerican cultures. Religions focused on what the cultures most valued, be it war or agriculture. The different cultures believed that human actions, such as sacrifices or proper behavior, could influence the actions of the gods.

Followers of these different cultures traded artifacts, ideas, and raw materials. Seashells from coastal areas and **obsidian** from the highlands traveled across Mesoamerica. Some villages grew from trade or religious centers into **city-states.** Skilled artisans made the cities beautiful, creating large stone buildings and spectacular **temples,** while talented farmers raised enough food to feed urban populations. But wars also broke out. Some were fought between rival cities of a single culture. Other wars erupted when different cultures vied for control of a region.

In A.D. 1250, the **Aztecs,** a group that had originated in northern Mexico, arrived in the Valley of Mexico. According to their myths, the Aztecs—guided by priests and their primary god, **Huitzilopochtli**—had wandered the deserts of northern Mexico for years before reaching the valley, where they founded the city of Tenochtitlán. A militaristic people who thrived on warfare and conquest, the Aztecs built an empire that lasted from 1430 to 1519. This story, set more than 500 years ago, tells about the residents of Tenochtitlán, a city that became one of the great urban centers of Mesoamerica.

Series Editors

PART ONE

THE WORLD OF THE AZTECS

(Right) *This map shows the modern-day nation of Mexico and the other nations that make up Mesoamerica. The Federal District of Mexico, in dark yellow, is where the Valley of Mexico, the heart of the Aztec world, is found. (Below left) Aztec artwork shows Aztec priests during their migration from Aztlán, the Aztecs' mythic place of origin, to the Valley of Mexico. (Below right) Located in a shallow area of Lake Texcoco, Tenochtitlán and Tlatelolco were connected to the mainland by broad causeways constructed by Aztec workers. A number of other city-states surrounded the lake.*

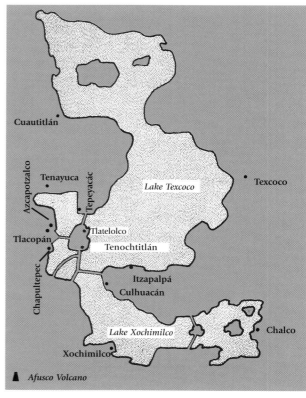

The Aztecs made their home in a mountain-ringed basin known in modern times as the Valley of Mexico. Although the present-day valley is dry, it was once a lush region filled with water. Rivers from the mountains flowed down into the valley. There were five connected lakes during the dry season. During the rainy season, the rivers and lakes flooded to make one large lake (Lake Texcoco). Fish and birds inhabited the lake, and animals such as deer and pumas populated the surrounding area. Protected by steep mountains, the Valley of Mexico was an ideal spot for settlement.

Belize

Honduras

Nicaragua

El Salvador

Costa Rica

Panama

(Top) The *modern-day megalopolis of Mexico City is located in the Valley of Mexico. It covers the territory once occupied by Lake Texcoco and the Aztec cities of Tenochtitlán and Tlatelolco.* (Top right) *An engraving from the Calendar Temple in Tlatelolco.* (Right) *This Aztec illustration tells the story of Tenochtitlán's founding. According to Aztec mythology, Tenochtitlán was born on a small, rocky island where an eagle, holding a serpent in its beak, sat on a cactus.*

The Aztecs, originally known as the Mexica, were one of many **Nahuatl**-speaking groups that moved into the Valley of Mexico in the thirteenth century. One of the last groups to arrive in the region, the Aztecs were considered outsiders by their neighbors. Each time the Aztecs settled, hostile groups drove them away. But in 1325, after wandering the basin for 75 years, the Aztecs founded the city of Tenochtitlán on a barren island in the middle of Lake Texcoco.

Soon the Aztecs began to trade with the other groups in the valley. Aztec traders offered fish, frogs, birds, and insects from the lake in return for wood and stone from mainland city-states. With these materials, the Aztecs built homes and constructed spectacular temples to their gods.

(Left) *Residents of Tenochtitlán paddled canoes along the canals that traversed the city.* (Below) *This reconstruction shows the holy grounds of Tenochtitlán. In the center background is the Great Temple, which had shrines dedicated to to the Aztec gods Huitzilopochtli and Tlaloc. Aztec priests performed human sacrifices at these shrines. Also on the grounds were temples dedicated to other Aztec gods and a military school for young soldiers.*

Workers drained shallow marshes and cut a grid of canals and streets. Farmers built island fields, known as *chinampas*, out of layers of mud and vegetation. They planted a variety of crops—maize, squash, chiles, and tomatoes—to feed the city's residents. Craftspeople and merchants sold their wares in the city's markets.

As the Aztecs prospered in Tenochtitlán, they became more involved with other groups in the basin. In 1428 they formed an alliance with the city-states of Texcoco and Tlacopan and began wars to conquer the other city-states of the valley. Eventually, Tenochtitlán dominated that alliance, and the Aztecs became the most powerful group in the Valley of Mexico. The other city-states in the valley came under Aztec rule.

Through warfare and conquest the Aztecs enriched the city of Tenochtitlán, which became the seat of the Aztec Empire. When the Aztecs conquered a city, the defeated residents had to pay a **tribute,** which could take many forms. Some residents gave the Aztecs items such as clothing and jewelry, while others served in the Aztec army or provided labor for construction. To feed Tenochtitlán's growing population, Aztec leaders also demanded crops and foodstuffs from conquered city-states.

Most important, conquest provided victims for sacrifice, a significant part of Aztec religious practice. The Aztecs believed that they were responsible for maintaining the order of the universe, which involved daily sacrifices of human blood to Huitzilopochtli and to other gods. To obtain victims for sacrifice, Aztec warriors tried to capture rather than kill their battlefield opponents. After a successful battle, Aztec soldiers brought captured warriors to temples, where priests sacrificed them to the gods.

Aztec society was divided into two large social groups—nobles and commoners. Each group had a defined role in Aztec society and lived by strict rules of behavior. The most powerful noble was the *tlatoani* of Tenochtitlán, who ruled the empire and organized the wars of conquest.

(Top) *An engraving of an Eagle Knight. Eagle Knights were highly skilled warriors who wore elaborate costumes made of eagle feathers.* (Following pages) *These two life-size Eagle Knight sculptures, made of stucco and terracotta, were found in the Hall of the Eagle Knights in Tenochtitlán. The illustrations of Aztec warriors are from an illustrated manuscript that contains the history of the Aztecs as recorded by a Spanish priest, Fray Bernardino de Sahagún, in the sixteenth century.*

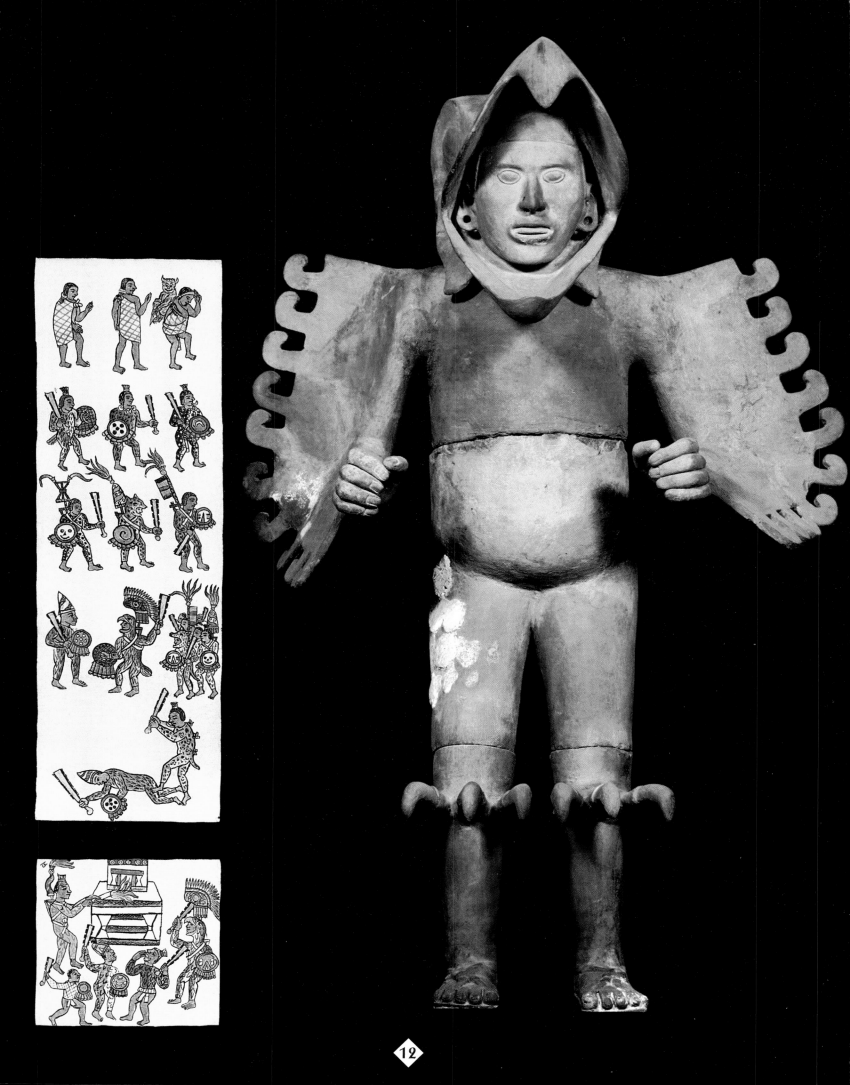

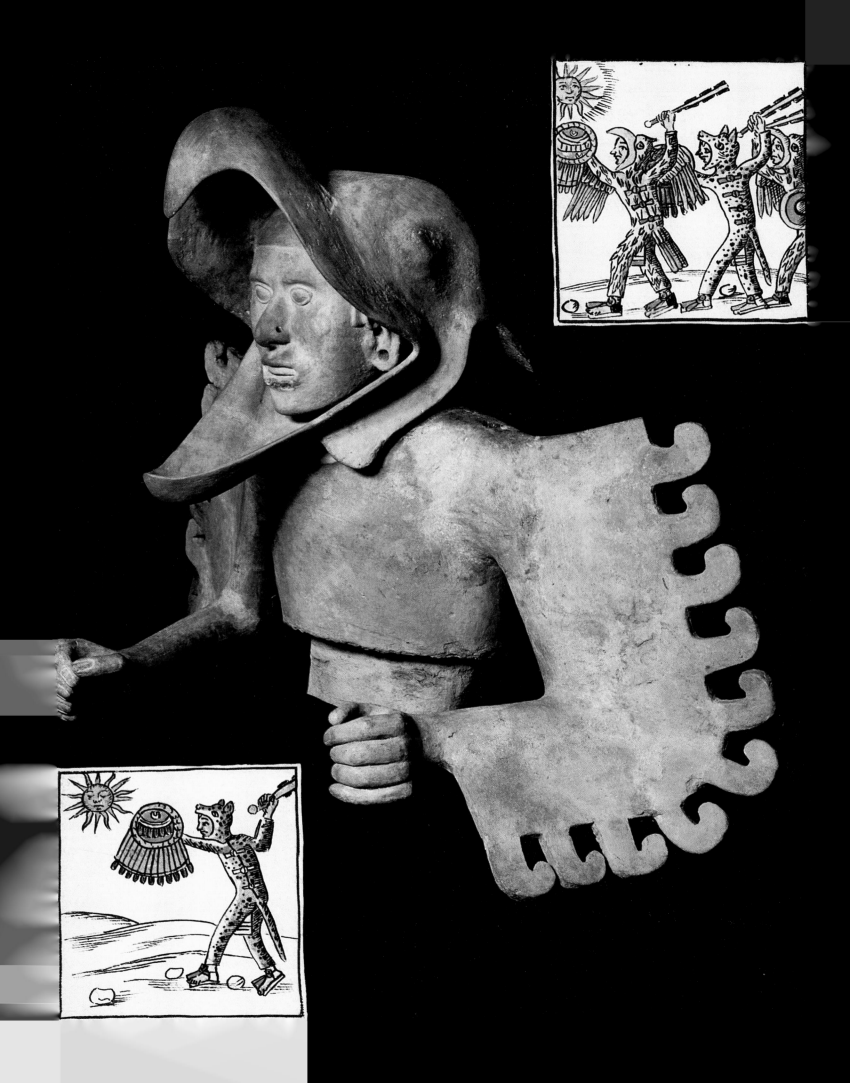

Below the tlatoani were nobles who ruled conquered city-states. Lesser nobles worked in the government, owned land, served as priests and teachers, and commanded the army. The commoners, who lived in districts known as *calpullis*, provided goods and services for nobles and served in the army. Merchants and artisans made up an intermediate group.

The roles of men and women in Aztec society were also strictly defined. Aztec men were landowners, artisans, farmers, fishers, priests, and merchants. Above all, Aztec men were expected to be courageous warriors. Whether noblewomen or commoners, Aztec women raised children, wove cloth, and prepared meals.

Because conquest enabled the Aztecs to build and sustain their empire, warfare became a primary focus of Aztec society. To ensure that they would maintain their military supremacy, Aztec boys were rigorously trained in military classes from a young age. In the *calmecac*, the sons of nobles received combat training and learned how to lead the army. In the *telpochcalli*, sons of commoners studied martial arts and the secrets of war. When the Aztecs went to war, all young men were expected to participate.

(Top) *This illustration shows Aztec students entering a telpochcalli. Each neighborhood in Tenochtitlán had one of these military schools. When the Aztecs went to battle, the army was divided into regiments made up of the members of a single telpochcalli.* (Above) ***Tezcatlipoca,*** *an Aztec god, was the patron god of the telpochcalli.* (Right) *The Aztecs decorated the rock basement of the Great Temple in Tenochtitlán with sculpted skulls, meant to represent the victims of sacrifice.* (Facing page) *Aztec warriors received gifts of clothing and headgear for capturing prisoners. As a warrior captured more prisoners, the clothing became more elaborate. The third character in the illustration, who captured four prisoners, earned a suit of jaguar skin. The last character is the noble military boss, who wears an elaborate feather headdress and a luxurious cape.*

The Role of Warfare in Aztec Society

Aztec war education emphasized earning honor through battlefield achievements. At the age of 10, young boys would have their head shaved, except for a single lock that was worn in a ponytail. If a boy was older than 15 and had not taken a prisoner in battle, he was subject to taunts of *"cuezpalchicapul"* (old ponytail). After a boy had captured an enemy warrior in battle, the ponytail could be cut off.

The capture of enemy warriors enabled Aztec men to rise in society. As a warrior captured more prisoners, he received greater honors. The warrior who took four prisoners by his own merit had the privilege of wearing a distinctive hairstyle—a tuft of hair on top of his head. Other honors included luxurious cloaks, earrings made out of precious stones, and special benefits in the army and the neighborhood.

All Aztec men wanted to be respected and admired for their courage in battle. The most able warriors remained dedicated for life to the army and became members of the Order of Eagle Knights or the Order of Jaguar Knights. Wearing elaborate costumes made of eagle feathers and jaguar skins, these warriors were the most feared in the Aztec army.

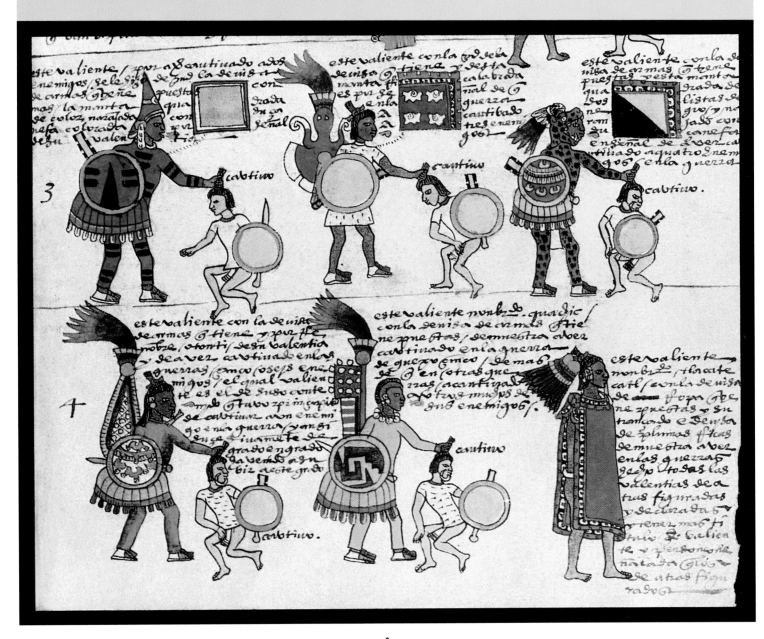

Tenochtitlán's ruins lie buried beneath modern-day Mexico City, but much is known about the city and its inhabitants. Some of this knowledge comes from the observations of the Spanish explorers who arrived in Tenochtitlán in 1519. In books and letters, Spanish soldiers and Catholic priests vividly described the city and the cultural practices of the Aztecs. They also drew maps and sketches of the city. Stone, wood, and metal artifacts uncovered by modern-day archaeologists add to the knowledge of Aztec beliefs and lifestyle. The **codices** created by Aztec priests (and later translated into Spanish by Catholic priests) are also a valuable source of information about the Aztecs. These picture manuscripts contain records of significant events in the history of the Aztecs and their great city. Codices also recorded religious beliefs and other aspects of Aztec life. Very few original codices remain, so historians learn about the Aztecs by studying reproductions of these documents.

Although the characters in this story are fictitious, the circumstances are real. Motecuhzoma (or Montezuma) Ilhuicamina, who became the Aztec leader in 1440, waged many wars to consolidate the power and wealth of the Aztec Empire. The battle described in this story took place during Motecuhzoma's campaign against the city-state of **Chalco,** which lasted for more than 20 years. The Aztecs sought to conquer the Chalcas—their most powerful rival—and to solidify their hold over the Valley of Mexico. They also wanted to gain access to the Chalcas' rich farmland. Before this battle, the Chalcas had killed Tlacahuepan, an Aztec noble. Let's travel back more than 500 years in time to spend a day with Icxitontli, a young Aztec warrior, as he prepares for the upcoming battle.

PART TWO

A Day With Icxitontli, An Aztec Warrior

From the heights of the temples, the ringing **tambores** announced the arrival of midday. A cool spring breeze rustled the ash trees and **ahuehuetes,** creating a soft murmur that traveled across the island. Walking down one of the narrowest streets of Tenochtitlán, Icxitontli hurried toward his parents' house on the southern bank of the island. In the center of the patio, Icxitontli's mother was grinding corn for the **nixtamal,** which she would use to make tortillas. Bent over the **metate,** she did not notice her son's approach. Icxitontli's father was trying to catch a turkey that had just jumped out of its pen. When he saw Icxitontli, the man ran over to his son and hugged him, saying, "You must be tired. Come, sit down."

In front of the door of the main room, Icxitontli and his father squatted face-to-face. It had been a long time since they had last seen one another. Icxitontli lived in the telpochcalli, the school dedicated to military training. He occasionally received permission from the principal to visit his parents. This could be for two distinct reasons. Sometimes the principal arranged for Icxitontli to eat in his house so that he could spend time with his parents. In that case, his mother would be hurrying to prepare a dish of whitefish wrapped in scented herbs. At other times, a visit meant the approach of a battle in which Icxitontli would have to take part.

The serious and worried look on the boy's face explained the motive for his visit. His father, a man of very few words, gave Icxitontli a little lecture. He reminded his son to be cautious of danger but at the same time to act valiantly.

He said slowly, "Take these words with you, that you may have courage, and that you might bring honor to this house."

After bringing him some water, Icxitontli's mother went back to the main bedroom and rekindled the fire. She sprinkled **copal** on the flame as an offering to the ancestral spirits who lived beneath the fire. She asked them to protect her son. This was a way for her to avoid the difficult good-bye, which was always full of tears.

After saying good-bye to his father and mother, Icxitontli left the house and walked quickly back to the telpochcalli. As he crossed a small, wooden bridge over the canal he felt a blow to the head, then another, and another. He almost lost his balance. Three objects fell on the planks of the bridge and rolled into the water. He saw that they were three hard orange *tejocotes* (small, round fruit).

Icxitontli turned his head and discovered three little boys, his neighbors, laughing at him. They shouted, "Cuezpalchicapul! Cuezpalchicapul!"

Without responding, Icxitontli continued walking. He tried to hide his embarrassment. At 17 years old, he had never taken a prisoner during a battle. The teachers of his telpochcalli made him wear a ponytail so that everyone would know he lacked courage.

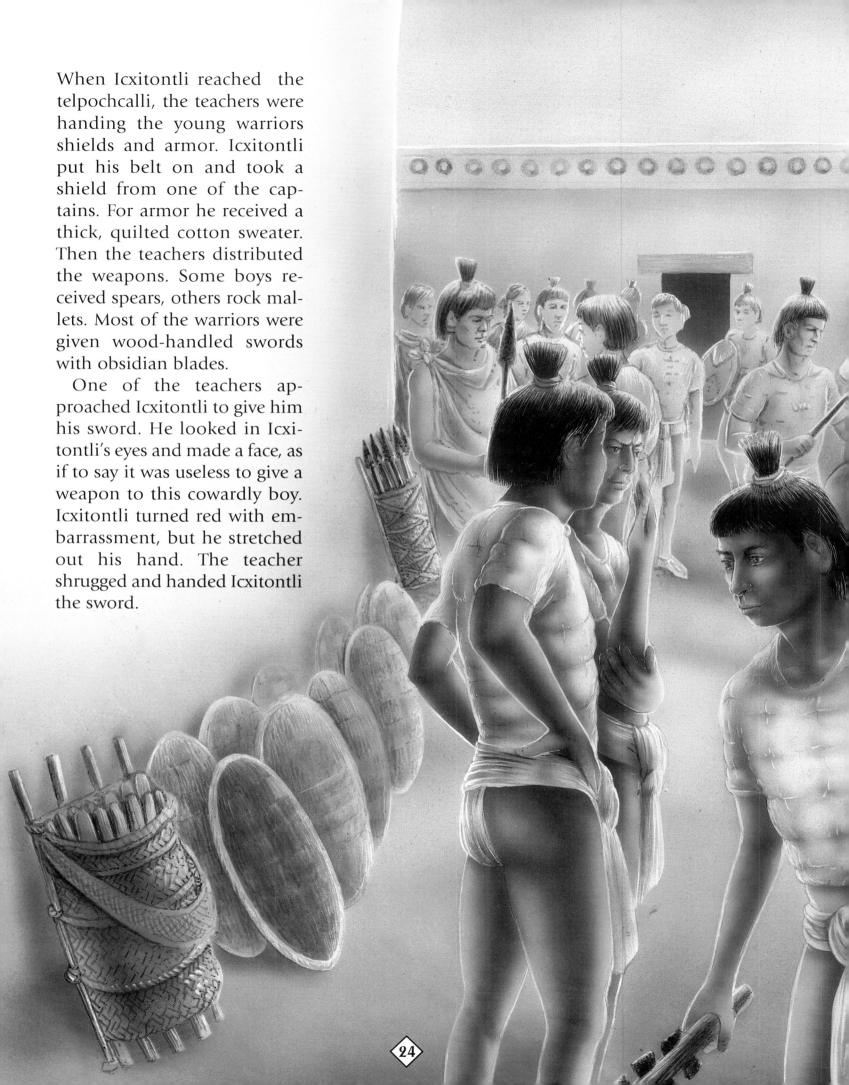

When Icxitontli reached the telpochcalli, the teachers were handing the young warriors shields and armor. Icxitontli put his belt on and took a shield from one of the captains. For armor he received a thick, quilted cotton sweater. Then the teachers distributed the weapons. Some boys received spears, others rock mallets. Most of the warriors were given wood-handled swords with obsidian blades.

One of the teachers approached Icxitontli to give him his sword. He looked in Icxitontli's eyes and made a face, as if to say it was useless to give a weapon to this cowardly boy. Icxitontli turned red with embarrassment, but he stretched out his hand. The teacher shrugged and handed Icxitontli the sword.

After all of the weapons had been passed out, the boys ate a light lunch of tortillas and beans in the patio of the telpochcalli. When they had finished, one of the army captains gave the boys instructions for the battle that was fast approaching. While another young warrior held up a codex, the captain explained the reason for the battle.

"Our Motecuhzoma has ordered a war to the death against the Chalcas, who have assassinated the noble captain Tlacahuepan," the captain said sternly.

In Icxitontli's imagination, the words of the captain mixed with unpleasant images. Closing his eyes, Icxitontli envisioned the three tejocotes floating in the canal and the long ponytail of a warrior without merit.

It was late afternoon by the time Icxitontli and the boys from the telpochcalli joined the other regiments of the Aztec army. They watched as the most accomplished warriors, the Eagle Knights and the Jaguar Knights, marched by at the front of the column. These ferocious warriors, who had been hardened by the clamor of many battles, would lead the army against the Chalcas. Icxitontli's regiment would follow in the rear.

The faces of the boys from the telpochcalli advertised their worry and nervousness. But the Eagle and the Jaguar Knights walked calmly and confidently in their elaborate costumes. Some were even chatting and joking. War was their job, and they had learned how to control their fear a long time ago. Icxitontli wondered if he would ever be one of these fierce warriors.

The sun was setting when the massive fighting force reached the outskirts of the city of Cuitláhuac. Icxitontli listened to the tambores that rang from the temples in the cities and villages of the valley, announcing the sunset. He saw market vendors leaving the town centers and the people of the surrounding villages preparing to return to their homes.

Along the banks of Lake Texcoco, people loaded their canoes with goods bought at the market. Their children gathered to watch the army. The flags rippled in front of each regiment, and the eye-catching suits and **insignias** in the forms of eagles and jaguars looked splendid in the fading light.

By the light of the moon, the army camped outside the village of Ayotzinco. They set up tents for the captains, then each squadron grouped around a bonfire. Icxitontli and some other boys were sent to the outskirts of the camp to watch for any possible movement by the enemy.

The campsite was calm when Icxitontli heard two *tecolotes* (owls), one on either end of the campsite, sing with voices that seemed almost human. The first thing they sang was "Valiant! Strong!" Then one bird sang "Cut! Cut!" and the other responded "Heart! Heart!" Then the first bird sang "Bloody Throat!" and the other replied "The Chalcas! The Chalcas!" Word of this good omen spread throughout the camp. Without a doubt, the Aztecs would triumph over the Chalcas.

Icxitontli unfolded the cloak he kept on his back during the journey. Looking to each of the four directions, he begged the god **Tezcatlipoca** to protect him during the upcoming battle.

33

The morning's first rays of light illuminated the Aztec army and sent long shadows across the field. In front of them lay Tlalmanalco, fortress and stronghold of the Chalcas. On the outskirts of the city, the Chalca warriors waited behind small log blockades.

The Aztec army formed a gigantic semicircle that advanced slowly, threatening to engulf the city. From the center of the formation, Icxitontli heard the grave lament of an ocean shell trumpet—the signal to attack. Using their bows, the Aztec warriors showered the Chalcas' blockades with arrows. Icxitontli watched as the volley of arrows forced the Chalcas to escape to the open countryside. When this occurred, the Aztec army advanced rapidly to attack their exposed and scattered enemy, maintaining their compact formation.

From a rise in the land, Icxitontli could see the battle unfold. The Eagle and Jaguar Knights raced into battle, engaging the Chalcas in combat. He could hear the cries and whoops of the warriors as the two armies fought fiercely. As the battle wore on, the Eagle and Jaguar warriors began to overwhelm the Chalcas with their superior fighting skills. While the Aztec army pushed forward, Icxitontli nervously waited for his turn to enter the battle.

Under the fierce mid-morning sun, Icxitontli's regiment entered into action behind the Eagle and Jaguar Knights. From there they passed to the front line quickly. By this point, the Chalcas were dazed. Many of their warriors had been captured, and others were retreating to Tlalmanaco. But Icxitontli knew that the danger was still enormous.

Icxitontli, his sword raised high in the air, raced forward into battle. But an enemy threw dirt in his face, forcing Icxitontli to pause and clear his eyes. When he reopened his eyes, he found himself surrounded by four Chalca warriors.

"Our women have the pots ready to cook you in chile!" shouted one of the warriors.

With the clarity of someone who feels lost, Icxitontli remembered the words of an old teacher from the telpochcalli: "If you have an enemy in front of you, attack him without respite. If you have two enemies, you also must be two people. Attack the first, and immediately turn to face the other. If you find yourself surrounded, be a whirlwind. Turn, turn, so that your ferocity has no limit."

Icxitontli whirled with his sword extended toward the abdomens of his adversaries, where their stiff cotton sweaters would be unable to protect them. Three fell wounded by Icxitontli's blows. The fourth bent over to avoid being cut by the slashing weapon but was hit in the head. The warrior fell to the ground, dazed and hurt.

By this time most of the Chalcas had fled the battlefield, and the Aztec army was on its way to destroy the temple of Tlalmanalco. Icxitontli realized that there were no more attackers around him. Guarding his victims, he waited for the younger boys from the back lines to arrive. These warriors, the youngest in the Aztec army, carried the ropes with which to tie up the prisoners.

Icxitontli asked one of the boys for four short ropes and one long one. With the short ropes, he bound the hands of his captives behind their backs. Then he took the long rope and wound it around each of their necks, linking them together. The wounded Chalcas, half-dead, did not resist.

Beneath the heat of the afternoon sun, the Aztec soldiers returned to Tenochtitlán victorious. The news had already circulated. Tlalmanalco was deserted. Half of the warriors had died in combat or had been captured. The other half had fled to the steep foothills of **Popocatépetl** with the other residents of the city in search of refuge.

In the neighboring town of Mixquic, the army had to walk a steep path. Stopping to rest, Icxitontli sat beneath a tree and gave custody of his prisoners to some warriors who had not fought in the battle. While relaxing, the young warrior felt something fall on his head. Then he felt another and another. Three tejocotes had fallen from the tree and rolled across the ground.

"I have captured four enemies. They will cut off my ponytail and give me a haircut of a valiant man. They will give me a cloth with insignias on it, and never again will they laugh at me when I walk down the street," said Icxitontli. He then lifted the ripest tejocote and bit into it. What a delicious fruit!

AFTERWORD

Tenochtitlán grew even more powerful after the victory over Chalco. The Aztecs began conquering cities beyond the Valley of Mexico. Eventually, the Aztec Empire stretched to the Gulf of Mexico, and Aztec culture dominated the region. In 1502 Tenochtitlán was nearly destroyed by a flood, but a ruler named Motecuhzoma II rebuilt the city, making it even more beautiful.

In 1519 the Spanish explorer Hernando Cortés and his fleet arrived in Tenochtitlán. The Spaniards admired the city and the many treasures it held, but they were disgusted by the Aztecs' practice of human sacrifice. They also wanted the Aztecs to give up their gods in favor of Christianity. In 1520 Cortés and his men took Motecuhzoma II prisoner, and war broke out between the two sides. In 1521 Cortés and his troops defeated the Aztecs and destroyed the city. With their victory, the Spaniards became the rulers of the Aztec Empire.

The Spaniards had the Aztecs and other native peoples build Mexico City upon the ruins of Tenochtitlán. Mexico City became the capital of New Spain, the Spanish colony that included territory in Mesoamerica and what would become the southwestern United States. Some Aztec nobles owned land and played a small role in the new government, but most Aztecs were enslaved by the conquerors. Many died from hardship and from European diseases such as smallpox.

Aztec culture changed over time. Catholic priests converted the Aztecs and other Nahuatl-speaking groups to Christianity. Most Aztec nobles adopted Spanish ways, but among other people the traditional Aztec beliefs and rituals did not completely die. Many Aztec traditions combined with Spanish ways to form the culture of modern-day Mexico. Some Mexicans of Aztec heritage still speak the Nahuatl language, and many towns and sites retain Aztec names. In recognition of the significance of the Aztecs, the modern-day Mexican flag depicts an eagle perched on a cactus with a serpent in its mouth.

GLOSSARY

ahuehuete: A tree that grows in swampy, humid areas in the southeastern United States and in Mexico. Its name means "old man of the water" in Nahuatl.

Aztecs: The people of Tenochtitlán and Tlatelolco, originally known as the Mexica. Historians also use the name to refer to the inhabitants of the Valley of Mexico who were conquered by the Aztecs and became part of their empire.

basin: A low place in the surface of the land, usually with a body of water occupying the lowest part.

calmécac: The school where the sons of Aztec nobles studied religion, government, the arts, public works, and the art of warfare. From this school graduated the future leaders of the Aztec world.

calpulli: A district within a town or city that was governed by an Aztec noble. Each calpulli had its own government, patron god, school, and land.

Chalco: A powerful city-state near the southern edge of the Valley of Mexico. Its inhabitants, the Chalcas, spoke the Nahuatl language. The city-state of Chalco had three capitals—Atenco, Tlalmanalco, and Amaquemecan.

city-state: A main city and its surrounding territory. Aztec city-states consisted of one major urban center and many smaller communities.

codex: A manuscript written with picture symbols that represented events and beliefs. Aztec **codices** recorded much of the history of the Aztecs and their empire.

copal: A type of incense (fragrant resin) frequently used in Aztec religious ceremonies.

Huitzilopochtli: The god of war and the primary Aztec deity.

insignia: A distinctive symbol made of paper or precious feathers that the highest-ranking soldiers wore on their uniform and headdress to indicate their rank. All of the regiments that participated in a battle wore a bandana with the insignia of their regiment.

Mesoamerica: An area that includes modern-day Honduras, Belize, Guatemala, El Salvador, and much of Mexico.

metate: A stone used to grind corn.

Nahuatl: The language spoken by the Aztecs and other groups in the Valley of Mexico. Nahuatl is still spoken by many modern-day Mexicans

nixtamal: A mixture of finely ground cornmeal and lime.

obsidian: Volcanic glass that was used to make needles, knives, swords, and other sharp objects.

Popocatépetl: A great active volcano situated in one of the mountain ranges that surround the Valley of Mexico.

tambore: A percussion instrument used to mark certain hours of the day, such as the sunset, and to announce the beginning of a battle. Tambores were also used during ceremonies and dances.

telpochcalli: A school that focused on the military education of young Aztec commoners.

temple: A large, pyramid-shaped stone structure with a flat roof. Aztec temples, which were dedicated to different gods, served as places of worship. Most Aztec sacrifices were performed on top of the Great Temple in Tenochtitlán.

Tezcatlipoca: A major Aztec god and the patron of the telpochcalli.

tlatoani: The supreme ruler or king of a city-state, region, or town.

tribute: A tax paid in products like corn, cacao beans, precious stones, manufactured goods, feathers, or through manual labor of varying tasks. The residents of conquered city-states were obligated to pay this tax to the Aztec government.

PRONUNCIATION GUIDE

ahuehuetes	ah-way-WAY-tays
Ayotzinco	ah-yoht-SEEN-coh
calmécac	kahl-MAY-kahk
calpulli	kahl-POH-lee
Chalco	CHAHL-coh
Culhuacan	kool-wah-KAHN
Huitzilopochtli	weet-see-loh-POHCH-tlee
Icxitontli	eek-shee-TOHN-tlee
Motecuhzoma	moh-tehk-ooh-ZOH-mah
Nahuatl	nah-WAH-tl
nixtamal	neesh-tah-MAHL
Popocatépetl	poh-poh-cah-TEH-peh-tl
tambores	tahm-BOH-rehs
tecolotes	teh-coh-LOH-tehs
tejocotes	teh-hoh-COH-tehs
telpochcalli	tehl-poch-CAH-lee
Tenochtitlán	tay-noch-tee-TLAHN
Texcoco	tesh-KOH-koh
Tezcatlipoca	tays-kah-tlee-POH-kah
Tlacopan	tlah-koh-PAHN
Tlamanalco	tlah-mah-NAHL-koh
Tlatelolco	tlah-teh-LOHL-coh
tlatoani	tlah-toh-AH-nee

FURTHER READING

Berdan, Francis F. *The Aztecs.* New York: Chelsea House Publishers, 1989.

Boone, Elizabeth Hill. *The Aztec World.* Montreal: St. Remy Press, 1994.

Cory, Steve. *Daily Life in Ancient and Modern Mexico City.* Minneapolis: Lerner Publications Company, 1999.

Linares, Federica Navarette. *A Day With a Maya.* Minneapolis: Runestone Press, 1999.

Mexico in Pictures. Minneapolis: Lerner Publications Company, 1994.

Time-Life Books. *Aztecs: Reign of Blood & Splendor.* Alexandria, VA: Time-Life Books, 1992.

Warburton, Lois. *Aztec Civilization.* San Diego: Lucent Books, 1995.

INDEX

ABOUT THE
AUTHOR AND THE ILLUSTRATOR

Pablo Escalante Gonzalbo has a Ph.D in history. He works as a researcher for the Institute of Aesthetic Investigations and as a professor in the Department of Philosophy and Art at the National Autonomous University of Mexico. His work covers daily life among the Nahuatl-speaking peoples on the eve of the Spanish conquest and indigenous art and culture of the sixteenth century. His previous books include *History of the New World* and *Education and Ideology in Ancient Mexico.* He has also authored many essays as well as chapters in textbooks.

Guillermo de Gante, a native of Veracruz, Mexico, has degrees in graphic design and advanced teaching in visual arts from the National School of Plastic Arts at the National Autonomous University of Mexico, where he also teaches. His illustrations have appeared in a number of books and periodicals.